WATER
FROM
THE ROCK

A N D R E W   S M I T H

WESTBOW
PRESS®
A DIVISION OF THOMAS NELSON
& ZONDERVAN

WestBow Press books may be ordered through booksellers or by contacting:

WestBow Press
A Division of Thomas Nelson & Zondervan
1663 Liberty Drive
Bloomington, IN 47403
www.westbowpress.com
1 (866) 928-1240

Scripture quotations marked (NLT) are taken from the Holy Bible, New Living Translation, copyright ©1996, 2004, 2015 by Tyndale House Foundation. Used by permission of Tyndale House Publishers, Inc., Carol Stream, Illinois 60188. All rights reserved.

Unless otherwise cited, all scripture taken from the King James Version of the Bible.

ISBN: 978-1-9736-5187-1 (sc)
ISBN: 978-1-9736-5188-8 (e)

Print information available on the last page.

WestBow Press rev. date: 02/11/2019

FOREWORD

Several years ago I put some of my writings into a little book called "Manna for the Journey" Since then I have committed more thoughts to writing and there were other early writings that were not included in the first book. Some writings in this publication are 50 years old and some were written in 2018.

I have been inspired and challenged by several pastors including Jack Prince, Brooks Ramsey, James Hatley, Joel Snyder, Roger Lovette, Hal Poe, Mike Smith, Brent Beasley and Stephen Cook. My early life was inspired by my father, John J. Smith and by A. Scott Patterson.

When my pen starts to write I sometimes do not know which of these men is the inspiration behind the writing.

The children of Israel needed both manna and water from the rock. I hope that these thoughts and musings provide sustaince for your journey through this life.

Andrew

PREFACE

Andrew Smith, Architect by trade, consistent Christian by conviction has blended creativity and faith in this collection of his God encounters. His thoughts are linked like beads on a necklace: different shapes of poetry and prose all of which are grounded by reality and hope. Each arises from private experiences and from gathered congregations. Many are stirrings stimulated by messages delivered by his pastors.

A word of warning – some are sticky and may remain with the reader far beyond a single reading.

Denny Spear
Pastor Emeritus
Dunwoody Baptist Church
Dunwoody, Georgia

Contents

Water From The Rock

"Then sang Moses and the children of Israel… I will sing unto the Lord, for he has triumphed gloriously.

Exodus 15.1

"and the people murmured against Moses,"

Exodus 17:3

"…and thou shalt smite the rock, and there shall water out of it, that the people may drink."

Exodus 17:6

When they were rescued, they sang and they danced.

Later they were complaining. They were tired and they were thirsty.

They had a problem.

They could not depend on the Egyptians to take care of them. They were not slaves anymore. They were free. They were on their own.

We are a lot like the Israelites. Our memories are selective. They can interfere with our need to get on with the task at hand.

Sometimes our mind go back to when so many people came to Second Baptist Church we could not seat them all. We were the new dynamic Baptist Church on the eastern edge of the city. But, we must not be held hostage by our history. Nostalgia can grab you and drag you down if you are not careful.

Now we are the established, traditional, moderate voice in the heart of the city.

We must cherish our past but we must look for new ways to minister, to serve, to love in the here and now.

Moses went forward and struck the rock. The water flowed. But not before he struck the rock with his staff.

Thanks be to God that nostalgia did not get the best of Moses and the children of Israel.

Thanks be to God that we can go forward with commitment and love.

PS: The first Sunday I visited Second Baptist Church, Memphis, Tennessee, in April of 1968, (two weeks after Martin Luther King was assassinated) there were policemen parking cars on Walnut Grove, the balcony was full, there were chairs in the aisles and people standing in the foyer who could not find a seat. The young pastor, Brooks Ramsey, preached a gospel of love and reconciliation. He proclaimed:

"God is no respecter of persons".

In 2018 our young pastor preaches that same message. If we need to get chairs we will get them, but whether we need them or not, he will continue to preach the all inclusive love of God to all persons. And Second Baptist Church will continue to minister to all persons regardless of circumstances.

Only Enough

"Then the Lord said to Moses, Behold, I will rain bread from heaven for you, and the people shall go out and gather a certain rate every day..."

Exodus 16:4

It wasn't that the plagues had not freed them.
It wasn't that the sea had not parted.
The problem was that today there was no food.

They were six weeks into the journey and they were hungry.

God heard their murmurings and provided manna, but for only one day at a time.

Sometimes it seems that God gives only the minimum we need to sustain us.

Sometimes it seems that we are given only minimum protection.

But always He gives us maximum grace.

Whatever the future may bring, God is leading us along the way.

All people, all congregations, are in between what they were and what they are going to be.

We are going forward.
There is no alternative.
The question is are we going forward with murmurings?
Or are we going forward in the love of God?

Remember the manna but get on with the rest of your life.

Believe

I must believe –
Whether I like where I am headed or not
Is secondary to the need to believe
That I am headed in the right way –

Which presumes that I know what is the right way. Which is
a rash assumption!

Still I must believe!

J oy

How do we define joy?

How does it compare to

> Happiness,
> Satisfaction,
> Gladness?

We feel happy,
We are satisfied,
We experience gladness.

Joy is deeper.
It wells up from within
It overwhelms us.

It is not sought,
It is not worked for,
It is not learned.

It happens,
Thank God,
It happens!

Then

The ponderous broom of history
Sweeping away all traces of
Individual lives motivates you
More than the hope
Of ten thousand Golden Statues
Or trumpets
Or coins.

Hugh Prather "Notes on love and courage"

When the overwhelming problems
Looming out there in the future
Render the history of individual lives
Into meaningless data

Who is going to care
Whether I loved or not?
Whether I was loved or not?
Who will know about the

Sacrifice
Discipline
Commitment
Loyalty
Devotion
Tenderness
Joy
Disappointment
Happiness
Grief

Who is going to care
When it is over;
When I too have become
Nameless and forgotten?

I don't know about then
But I do know about now!

I care!

God Is So Good!

I heard her on the telephone talking to one of her long time friends. After they had chatted back and forth for several minutes I heard her say:

"I know that she is sick and old, (they were talking about her friend's mother-in-law) but you simply have to remember all that she did for you. When you were so sick for such a long time she took care of you."

"I know that it's tough for you now but when tough times come to me I simply remember the little song that we teach the three year old children in Sunday school."

> "God is so good,
> God is so good,
> God is so good,
> He's so good to me."

That is it!

It is so simple!

It is so true!

God is so good
And he has been so good to us!

Praise God from whom all blessings flow!

Feathers

"He will cover you with his feathers and under his wings you will find refuge."

Psalm 91:4

Several years ago the Ladies Bible Study Group
Studied the 91st Psalm at their Tuesday morning meeting.

On the way home one of the ladies stopped at a traffic light.
A man forced his way into her car,
Brandished a gun in her face and demanded her money.

The lady began to frail her arms
And scream,

"Feathers,
Feathers,
Feathers".

After a while the man said,
"Lady, you are crazy!"
And got out of the car and ran away.

Under his wings you will find refuge!"

E clecticism

Just as architecture must reflect with boldness the character and technology of today, theology must reflect with boldness the character of God revealed in the language of today.

Eclecticism in theology is just as foolish as eclecticism in architecture.

God's revelation is Jesus Christ 2000 years ago has no meaning unless it becomes real in the lives of people today.

Doors

Lord you know that I have never
Shied away from open doors.
In fact, I have always bounded through open doors
With the gusto of Poo's friend Tigger!

It is standing here looking at all these closed doors
That is giving me a problem.
How can I maintain any semblance of peace?
When my very soul is screaming
Open! Open! Open!
Now! Now! Now!

Help me to remember
That doors that are forced open
Are prone to bring pain and disappointment.

Help me to remember
That you have opened doors for me
Many times before.

Help me to remember
That I have never gone through
Those doors alone.

You know Lord,
That we who are by nature
And training
Men and women of action
Find it difficult to wait with patience.

I know that at the proper time
The door will open
And I will go in with joy and confidence
But in the meantime
Please draw near
For only your presence
Can quell the turmoil that rages within.

Daily

*"If any man will come after me, let him deny himself,
and take up his cross daily and follow me."*

Luke 9:23

Jesus said that the highest ethic of man is to give his life for
someone else.

He intensified the concept by saying that the sacrifice must be
offered daily.

It is only when the drive for your own desperate needs comes
in conflict with the needs of others that you know the reality
of daily sacrifice.

The sacrifice of giving your life away has far more meaning
when you are old enough to count the years that remain.

Only when you consider the fact that tomorrow may never
come does the value of today's sacrifice have meaning.

Confidence

Help us to always look forward,
Confident that Jesus
Has prepared the way
By living it himself,
Victoriously.

Communion

Thank you Jesus
For the time we spend
At your table,
Where we are forced
To look deep into
The recesses of our souls.

Help us to know
That in that depth
We always find You.

Teach us
That real joy
Springs from the center
Of our being
Where we are united
With You.

On the surface we touch –
In depth we commune.

Help us
To take ourselves seriously,
To treat those we love tenderly,
And to love you passionately.

Fill us with the joy
Of encounter with you,
That we call Communion.

Choices

We deceive ourselves
Into thinking that we are not able
To make the choices we want to make!

Consideration must be given,
So many responsibilities,
So many people!

Yet on the other hand,
We do make the choices we want to make.
We could run away –

Others have done it –
They do it every day –
They simply walk out and never look back.

We don't do that –
And to be honest
We don't do it because we choose not to do it!

So I suppose it is true –
We do make the choices we want to make –
Or is it that we have already made them?

Wait

Our dreams,
Our hopes,
Our aspirations,
Our plans
Can in time turn out all wrong.

Somehow,
Somewhere,
Someway,
Something happens
And everything is changed.

A mistake?
An error?
A foolish decision?
On the other hand it may not be anything you have done.

Sometimes we do the very best we can do
And it is not enough!
Sometimes change is forced upon us
And there is nothing we can do about it.

God is in the business of making something good
Out of something bad.
Get ready for an invasion of God's love.

Do not make demands.
Do not make conditions.

Wait in God's time.

U<u>nique</u>

Share that which is unique
In your life.

Whatever the essence
Of your being is –
Allow it to be sanctified
By the presence
Of the Eternal
And you will share it with others –
Just like Paul shared
His Damascus road experience
With everyone he met.

Patience

Patience does not make things happen faster.
Patience does not change the outcome of events.

Patience counterbalances anxiety.
Patience is the evidence of faith.
Patience is trust personified.

Trust is faith in action.
Love is trust in action.
Hope is love in action.
Patience is hope in action.

Patience does not mean
No thinking,
No planning,
No analysis.

Patience means confidence.
Patience defuses time.
Patience tames the terrible prepositions;

Why?

When?

What?

What if?

Patience changes fear into joy!

The Little White Van

Early on Sunday mornings
You can see many kinds of vans
Scurrying around the city
Picking up well dressed ladies
And taking them to their houses of worship.

Little ladies with
Gray hair adorned with passé hats,
Stooped shoulders draped with white shawls
And tear stained Bibles seen through cataract glasses.

Little ladies with memories
Of youth forever vanished,
Lovers long gone
And children far removed.

Little ladies who struggle with loneliness
And battle with fear
In the midst of their intense desire
To remain valuable in the Kingdom of God.

Scarcely do they know how valuable they are.
They show us how to pray for the impossible
And make it come true,
How to live with joy in the blessings of one more day
And how to laugh in the face of the Devil himself
And grow old with dignity and grace.

Oh, how I love to drive the little white van
Around the city on Sunday mornings,
To pick up little gray haired ladies
and bring them to God's house
and there-by say in my own feeble way,

"Mother I love you."

This was written when I was driving the van for Second Baptist Church, in the late 1970's. Now, cataract glasses have been replaced by implants and many of the church vans have been sold because they were deemed unsafe. But tear stained bibles and white haired ladies who know how to pray are still with us.

Andrew

Time

In this age of scientific precision –
When the movements of the far reaches
Of the universe are charted
To mere fractions of a second,

It is significant that time
That is truly important is never measured by the chronograph
Or disciplined by the metronome.

When time has been tempered by the reality of life
And steeped by the emotions of the heart
Normal rhythms and pace get out of synch
And some seconds last longer than others.

There is no rational for the compression of time
That can make our earliest memories as fresh as yesterday
Or for the elongation of time
That can make one tender moment last a lifetime.

Like the three second kiss
That is tasted for fifty years
Or the single smile of acceptance

That beams forever like the light of an eternal
flame.

Like the month long days
That never seems to end
The week before the wedding vows
Are spoken.

Like the decade spend in the little room
At the front of the church
Waiting for the musical cue that will beckon you
To come out and see your bride walk down
the aisle.

Like the minute it takes for a babe in arms
To grow into a teenager
Flushed with the joy
Of being in love for the first time.

Like the day that passes so quickly
In which your parents change
From vigorous providers and protectors
Into sage but enfeebled elders of the tribe.

Like the year that flies by so swiftly
Between the wedding and the silver anniversary
And the year or two more
Until silver turn to gold.

Thank you God for giving us hearts
That sustains us when time stands still
And enshrines forever time
That sanctifies our very existence.

Walking On Water

"Jesus constrained his disciples to get into a ship and go before him to the other side. But the ship was tossed with waves."

Matthew 14:22 and 24

When you are busy with your daily tasks,
When you are struggling with the trials of life,
When the storms of life threaten your very soul,
Keep your eyes fixed upon Jesus.

It does not matter whether you are in the boat
Or in the water if you are in the middle of a storm.
It does not matter whether or not you are asked to walk on water,
If you keep your eyes fixed upon Jesus.

Sometimes it is more difficult to wait and trust
Than it is to try an impossible task,
But when it is time to wait, wait.
When it is time to walk, walk.
But keep your eyes fixed on Jesus.

Suffering And Hope

"We stand and rejoice in hope of the glory of God. And not only so, but we glory in tribulations also: knowing that tribulation worketh patience; And patience, experience, and hope."

Romans 5:2-4

It is in our suffering that we find hope.
If we did not know suffering we would not need hope.
Hope allows us to hear the music in our suffering.

When God's love has been poured into our hearts by the power of the Holy Spirit,
We understand that our suffering is not a tragedy to be endured
But a journey to be experienced.

Hope always comes to the surface of our lives.
We boast in our suffering.
We boast in our hope.

S ell It!

"Take thine ease, eat, drink and be merry."

Luke 12:19

"Sell what you have and give alms.."

Luke 12:33

The rich fool filled his barns...
Ignored his neighbors and lost it all...

Consider the Ravens...
Consider the Lilies...
Seek the Kingdom...

Fear not...

What a wonderful lesson about the providence and love of God, but what are we going to do about verse 33?

"Sell what you have!"
There must be something wrong!
"Sell what you have!"

It doesn't matter whether you have little or much,
to sell what you have reduces every person to poverty.

What can he mean? Surely he can't mean that we should sell
everything we have and give the money to the poor!

The problem with the rich fool was that his barns were full of
goods which dominated his life.

Jesus said that we must get rid of everything that keeps us from
doing our task in the Kingdom of God!

Sell it!

To Peter, James, John and Andrew he said,
Forget about your boats and nets!

If it is keeping you from working in the Kingdom
Get rid of it!

Sell it!

To us Jesus says, Forget about your possessions,
They are keeping you from being what you were meant to be,

They are keeping you from serving in the Kingdom.
Get rid of it!

Sell it!

How could this commandment of Jesus apply to us?
Not the house!
Not the cars!
Not the savings!

Surely he doesn't mean the toys!
The boat?
The golf clubs?
The guns?
The TV?

We certainly do not read his commandment that way.
Perhaps we simply skip verse 33!

> *"Where your treasure is, there will be your heart also."*
>
> *Luke 12:34*

Flesh And Blood

"...the Word was made flesh and dwelt among us,..."

John 1:14

I have read that there is a problem in medicine called the blood/brain barrier. It is important in diseases of the brain like Parkinson's and Alzheimer's.

Medicine carried by blood can not get through the brain's protective barrier. The problem goes untreated because of the barrier.

I think there is a flesh and blood barrier that keeps the Spirit of God from getting to the parts of our souls that need help.

There is something in our humanity that puts a barrier between us and the Spirit of God.

It takes a lot of prayer and humility to soften the barrier.

In fact:

It takes a miracle for the Spirit of God to get through the flesh and blood barrier.

Help us, Oh God, to pray for that miracle!

Help us to remember that God is in the miracle business.

Let the Word dwell among us.

A Certain Man

"A certain man went down from Jerusalem and fell among thieves…"

Luke 10:30

Who was the man who fell among thieves?
We are told something about the others:

> A Priest,
> A Levite,
> A Samaritan.

But who was the man who was robbed?

Was he a Jew?
Was he a Samaritan?
Was he rich?
Was he poor?
Was he young?
Was he old?

We don't know.

Jesus only said, "A certain man."

It didn't matter who he was.

It only mattered that he was in need!

Jesus did not tell us why the Priest and the Levite passed by.

They simply passed by.

They may have had very good reasons.

Jesus did not condemn them.

He simply said that the man who helped the man in need

Showed the love of God and was thereby a good neighbor.

The fact is that we are all Priests and Levites who pass by

And we are all Samaritans who stop and help.

And,

When we stop and help we show the love of God,

And,

When we pass by we miss an opportunity

To show the world that the love of God abides in our hearts.

Opportunity!

That is the lesson!

We must be careful to take advantage of the opportunities that come our way.

That is the only way we have to love our neighbors.

That is the only way we have to love God.

Wherever He Leads

"And everyone that hath forsaken houses, or brethren, or sisters, or father, or mother, or wife, or children, or lands, for my name's sake...shall inherit everlasting life."

Matthew 19:29

My father was the pastor of a nice suburban church. He and my mother had recently moved into a new house. Their children were grown. She was about as settled as a pastor's wife could be. There were only two problems; she could sing "Wherever He Leads I'll Go" and her husband was on a preaching mission in California.

When he came home he said, "Girtie, God is calling us to a small mission in California." She said, "John, are you sure?" He replied, "Girtie, we have always wanted to be foreign missionaries but we don't have enough education. There are more lost people in California than there are in some foreign countries." A week later they were gone!

They loaned, gave away or sold their furniture, stored, trashed or burned the papers and the 25 years of junk they couldn't pack into the trunk and the back seat of a 1956 Plymouth and headed west.

She said good bye to her aged and senile mother, her brothers and sisters, her eldest son and his family, her middle child and his new bride, her pregnant daughter and her husband and perhaps the most painful of all, her only grandchild.

She didn't realize that she was a living example of Matthew 19:29 but she did know how to sing, "Wherever He Leads I'll Go,"

You have to be careful when you sing, "Wherever He Leads I'll Go."

I wonder how many of us are willing to sing it – and mean it?

> *Help us, Our Father, to long to do thy will. Teach us to look for ways to give our lives away for others.*

Glasses

"Thus says the Lord: In the place where dogs licked up the blood of Naboth, dogs will also lick up your blood."

How can we look at this gross, harsh, bloody, gory, disgusting Old Testament story with "Cross" colored glasses?

What does it say to us? How can it relate to relatively sophisticated modern Christians? Surely we are too cultured to apply this Old Testament justice to the events of today.

Perhaps it says:

> That arrogance, conceit and the abuse of power is wrong no matter when it happens.

> That God's people have a responsibility to stand up for what is right, even if the stand is not popular.

That God, not man, is responsible for providing the means of retribution.

That in due time the penalty will be paid.

We must remember that the cross did not end violence. The cross was in its self the most violent event in the history of mankind but it was the tomb – the empty tomb – that proved that the love of God is more powerful than all the violence man can inflict on man and all the violence man can inflict on God!

Can we look at these violent Old Testament stories with "Cross" colored glasses? Yes we can and when we do we know that nothing, not the even the most horrible stories in all of history, nothing can separate us from the love of God. The cross says it all.

"Lord, do not let us forget that the cross changed everything!"

Free

"You will know the truth and the truth will make you free."

John 8:36

FREE! The word literally jumps out of the page. Freedom is such an integral part of our heritage, our existence, our culture, and our dreams that the word free has a power shared by few other words. Ingrained in our minds are the words from the Gettysburg Address, "that this Nation under God, shall have a new birth of freedom" and we still hear the echoes of Dr. King's exclamation of joy, "Free at last, Free at last, thank God Almighty we are free at last."

FREE! To be free. Free from sin, from doubt, from fear, from guilt, from pain, from oppression, from discrimination, from despair, from poverty, and from many, many other negative words.

FREE! And what is the TRUTH that will make us free? Note that it is truth - God's truth -

> "if you continue in my (Jesus') word... the truth
> shall make you free."

How can we contemplate the truth of God and not fall into the trap of esoteric thoughts; the trap of self-righteous phases that have very little to do with the reality of life?

We must remember that his truth was as much what he did as it was what he said. Only later did those first century disciples know that his truth meant Calvary. Only later did they know what, "take up your cross and follow me" meant. Only later did they know the meaning of the word sacrifice.

The truth will make you free. The truth will give you the freedom to give up your life for others. Do we really want to know that kind of truth? Do we really want that kind of freedom?

> Lord, help us to want the freedom revealed by
> your truth!

F<u>orgive</u>

"Then hear thou in heaven..and forgive...and give
to every man according to his ways, whose heart thou
knowest;"

I Kings 8:37-43

There are many people in this world who are not comforted by
the thought that God knows what is in our hearts. Even those
of us who appear to be "good Christians" have a dark region
that we would like to hide from God. Why then should King
Solomon be glad that God knows what is in our hearts?

Because the active word in this passage of Scripture is "forgive".
Our God is a forgiving God!

That is the most incredible message of the entire Bible. God
knows, but he forgives! That doesn't mean that we can be
irresponsible but it does mean that we can live with joy! He
knows but he understands. He forgives!

The entire mission of Jesus was to show us this basic truth. The birth, the life, the miracles, the parables, the sermons the death, the resurrection, the ascension, everything, everything in the life of Christ was to show us that our God is a forgiving God!

He knows but he forgives!

Isn't it wonderful that we have a forgiving God.

Dixieland

"Have mercy upon me, O Lord, for I am in trouble...."
"Blessed be the Lord: for he hath showed me his marvelous kindness..."

Psalm 31:9 and 21

Do you think that Psalm 31 was David's equivalent of a New Orleans funeral march? It starts out at a normal tempo but as the march progresses toward the cemetery it gets slower and slower. You can hear the style of the music change. Eventually it is pure blues.

David compounds his sorrow line upon line. It seems as if every verse ends in a flattened chord. *"I am in trouble."* *"My life is spent with grief"*. *"My strength faileth me"*. *"I am like a broken vessel"*. You can hear the reedy vibrato of the saxophone and the slide of the trombone moving down to a low note.

But then the trumpet and the clarinet start their interplay of melody and counter melody. *"Oh how great is thy goodness"*. *"He sheweth me his marvelous kindness"*. *"Love the Lord all ye his saints."* *"Be of good courage"*. The tempo quickens. The key changes.

Flats become sharps. The music brightens. The dance begins. The trumpet begins to play the high notes. The runs on the clarinet end in notes above the staff. It is the same song but the sound is completely different.

Isn't that the way it is with all of life. It is how we play the music that makes the difference. How wonderful are his mercies!

Let's dance!

> *Help us to remember that you are with us in all life,*
> *both the blue times and the bright times.*

Conduit

> *"We cannot keep from speaking about what we have seen and heard."*

> *Acts 4:20*

This verse reminds us of the story about Balaam's donkey:

> *"And the Lord opened the mouth of the ass, and she said unto Balaam, what have I done unto thee?*

> *Numbers 22:28*

Or the statement of Jesus:

> *"I tell you, if these were silent, the stones would shout out."*

> *Luke 19:40:*

The question is not, "Will the message of the love of God be proclaimed?" The question is, "Are we willing to be the conduit of that message?" Are we willing allow the scale, the deposits, the clogged up areas in our pipes to be cleaned out?

Can we get ourselves out of the way so that the message can get through?

We don't have to provide a pump – no big turbine – no booster of any kind – just a pipe – a conduit.

The miracle is that "we" don't even have to clean out the pipes. We simply have to allow the love of God to flow through a small opening, the "Yes to God", opening in our pipes. When God's love starts to flow, love will do the cleaning. Love will do the work and there will be a double blessing. A blessing will be received by those to whom love is given and to those who provide the pipe.

Isn't that incredible! The great reservoir of God's love – the cross – depends on our scaly and clogged up pipes in order for the message – the Gospel – the Good News to get through to mankind.

> Lord let me be a conduit of your love.
>
> or in more colloquial language
>
> Lord, Clean my pipes.

Worthless?

"...two blind men sitting by the wayside, when they heard that Jesus passed by, cried out, saying, have mercy on us, O Lord, thou son of David."

Matthew 20:30

Two blind men sitting by the side of the road. Hopeless, destitute, hopeless, poor, ragged, worthless, a drain on society.

The prophet and his entourage: How many? Twelve? Twenty? Fifty? More? It was probably more like that entourage of a rock star than it was like the image most of us have in our minds. The image of a holy man quietly walking along the road with a few friends. Remember, they were going to Passover. There thousands and thousands of people making their way to Jerusalem. People, children, animals. It could have been more like a Mardi Gras parade!

Why, in the midst of this mass of humanity did Jesus stop to listen to the cries of two blind beggars? Would the addition of two men with new sight (but still ragged, destitute and poor) make any impact on the new kingdom of God?

But; Jesus had compassion on them. He stopped and healed them.

"and they followed him".

How far? How long? Did they become disciples? Did they wave palm branches at the triumphal entry? Were they at the cross? Were they part of the five hundred at the ascension? Were they two of the hundred and twenty in the upper room? We do not know. The New Testament does not mention them again. They were obviously not important to the early church.

Were we not like the blind men. Helpless, hopeless and spiritually destitute when Jesus found us? Did we not ask for healing and did he not stop and heal us?

Let us follow him!

S ent

"Go your ways: Behold I send you forth as lambs among wolves."

Luke 10: 3

"And the seventy returned again with joy, saying, Lord, in your name even the demons submitted to us!"

Luke: 10:17

How many thousand actual words were condensed into that one sentence?

"Lord, ...the demons submitted to us!"

You can almost hear their breathless excitement. They probably sounded like a gaggle of geese!

Who were the 70 "Others" who were "sent" into the countryside to demonstrate the power of God? What happened to them? Why do we not hear a single thing about them in all the rest of the Gospel story?

Surely they were impressed. How could they go back home and act as if nothing had happened? How could people who had seen the power of God demonstrated in such a dynamic and powerful way not become disciples?

Perhaps the verbs give us a hint. He "called" some to be disciples and he "sent" others to cast out demons. Perhaps there were very practical reasons; Remember, if every fisherman had left his nets there would have been no fish to eat. Perhaps a band of 82 disciples would have drawn too much attention. The fact is that we do not know what happened to those 70 people.

What we do know is that he "sent" the 70 out - they went - they did what they were told to do - and they were astounded by their success,

And,

They had no idea how successful they had been!

Jesus said,

> *"I watched Satan fall from heaven like a flash of lighting."*
>
> *Luke 10:18*

They thought they had simply cast out a few demons!

They didn't know.

And neither do we!

When we do what we are "sent" to do and we do it in the name of the Lord we have no idea how much actually happens!

O gracious Enabler, multiply our feeble efforts with your power.

M ary's Perfume

"Then Mary took expensive perfume and poured it on Jesus' feet…"

John 12:3

"…and began to wash his feet with tears, and did wipe them with the hairs of her head, and kissed his feet, and anointed them with the ointment."

Luke 7:38.

Why did she do it?
Why did she anoint his feet with expensive oil?
Why did she use a resource worth a year's wages
on such a symbolic gesture?

Why did she make such a public expression of devotion?
Why did she risk ridicule and scandal?

She did not know how Jesus would respond!
What if he had rebuked her?
After all it was a lot of money.

Wasn't there some other way
she could say that she loved him?

We do not know the answer to any of these questions.

We only know that:

> Love that costs nothing has no meaning.
> Love that risks nothing has no value.

What she did
was not logical
was not sensible.

What she did
was an outpouring of unconditional love
was an irrational expression of devotion.

What is our response to the love of Jesus?

Can we risk like Mary?
Can we give like Mary?
Can we love like Mary?

Yes we can.

We can if we throw caution to the wind
and worship our Lord
without reservation
without doubt
without fear!

Behold How He Loved Him

"Jesus wept."

John 11:35

Why did Jesus weep at the tomb of Lazarus?
Had he not delayed his visit
so that the power of God could be demonstrated?
Did he not know that Lazarus would be raised from the dead.
Why did he weep?

Some have suggested that he knew that even after this miracle
the Jews would still refuse to believe.
Perhaps he knew that nothing would stop the acceleration of
events that would end at the cross.

It could be that real sorrow comes unbidden
in spite of all our resolve to not break down.
We all know that thinking about and understanding tragedy
does not hold back sorrow. Maybe it was because he knew
that Lazarus would not use his second chance wisely.
Have you noticed that there is no record of anything
that Lazarus did after he was raised from the dead.

As far as we know, not a one of the people who Jesus healed made a significant contribution to the early church.
Not a one of the countless people who heard the master say, "Go and sin no more" became an apostle or an evangelist or a writer.

They were apparently common ordinary people with ordinary lives and they took their new lease on life and used it in common ordinary ways.

Jesus did not make radical change a prerequisite for healing. People needed healing, so Jesus healed them.

Why did he weep at the tomb of Lazarus?

Who knows - except that sorrow - sorrow that expresses itself with weeping, comes unbidden - it happens - it wells up from within - unwanted - unexpected.

Perhaps it is enough to know that he cared.
Cared for a friend in the common ordinary way
that we all care for those we love.

"Behold how he loved him!"

John 11:36

R emember Me

"And he took bread and gave thanks and brake it and gave unto them saying, this is my body which is given for you: this do in remembrance of me."

Luke 22:19

Our memories are selective.
Our memories are revealing.
Our memories are connective.
One memory leads to another.
Our memories say a lot about us.

Jesus said, "Remember me".
Remember my love.
Remember my forgiveness.
Remember that the grace of God has invaded your lives.
Remember that your lives have been changed by the love of God.

One of the saddest statements I have ever heard
is a line in a song by Willie Nelson.

*"Old worn-out saddles and old worn-out memories
with no one and no place to stay,"*

Help us to remember that memories that become blessings
Are not dependent on circumstances.
The joy of life is not a matter of good times,
It is a matter of the love of God and
What we allow that love to do in our lives.

"My Hero's have always been Cowboys,"

Sharon Vaughn

P<u>eace</u>

"O my father, if it be possible, let this cup pass from me:..."

Matthew 26:39

The peace of God has nothing to do with conditions!
It has everything to do with perception.

It is not the height of the waves,
It is the fear of the waves
That paralyzes the soul.

We therefore must not pray for a change in conditions!

To pray for a change in conditions
is to be irresponsible
in our relationship to others –

Our condition is never solitary.
It is always in communion with others;
Therefore a change in our condition
Also changes the condition of others.

That may or may not be good –
In fact, we can be sure
That those desperate pleas for change
That stem from the fear
That invades our souls
Will generate more trouble
Than we already have.

We can; however, pray for a change in perception.

The prayer in the Garden of Gestheme
For a change in conditions –
"Let this cup pass from me."
Did not change the fact of the cross.
But the change in perception
"Thy will be done."
Changed a common cross
Into the most extraordinary event in history,
CALVARY.

Silence

"O my father, if it be possible, let this cup pass from me..."

Matthew 26:39

What do you do when God is silent?

Sometimes it seems that the normal condition is silence.
Or is it that we do not know how to listen.

On the other hand you must be careful if you hear a voice.
You never know who might be speaking to you.

In any case silence is not an excuse for inaction.
It may be that God is waiting to see what you are going to do.

We can wait for God's assurance before we act.
Or we can act and trust that God will be with us all the way.

Remember Soren Kirkegaard's concept of
"A leap of faith into the darkness."

Seldom do we feel the power of God in inaction.
Action is an integral part of power.

Even Jesus did not get an answer in the Garden
But that did not keep him from his destiny, the cross.

That did not mean that God was absent
It only meant that he was silent.

The sacrifice for our salvation was made even if he did feel
"Forsaken".
But when he committed his spirit into the hands of his father,
his father was there.

He had been there all along.

So, what do we do?
We go.
We act.
We work.
We trust.
We Leap!

And we do not worry about silence.

Whose Image?

"Shew me the tribute money. …..Whose is this image…?"

Matthew 22:10-20

Render unto Caesar the things that are Caesar and
Render unto God the things that belong to God.

We know that the coin belongs to Caesar.
The question is, "What belongs to God?"

We know how to give our coins to Caesar.
But how do we give what belongs to God?

All that we are belongs to God.
It is a lot easier to give our coins than it is to give our all.

The giving of our all is never a one time gift.
Our all must be given over and over and over again.

It must be given regardless of its condition.
It must be given with all of its scars and deficiencies.

The question is not whose image is on the coin.
The question is whose image is on our souls.

Lifted Up

> *"And I, if I be lifted up from the earth, will draw all men unto me."*
>
> *John 12:32*
>
> *"But when the fullness of the time was come, God sent forth his son,...."*
>
> *Galatians 4:4*

Is it the lifted up aspect of the cross that makes it significant?

Does the fact that the cross was the method of execution in the first century have something to do with the fullness of time.

Of course there were many other factors: a common language, the Roman peace, the ease of transportation. There were many things that made the first century the "time" for the Christ event to occur.

Forty years later, after the Jewish rebellion, the Christ event could not have happened. The Jews were scattered to the four winds of the earth. The whole Jewish establishment that put Jesus to death did not even exist.

Earlier, before 40 BC when Judea was conquered by the Romans, the Christ event could not have occurred. If the Roman government had not been in control of the land the method of execution would have been stoning. Stephen was stoned.

The cross was used for secular, political crimes.

It was a complicated, contorted chain of events that put Jesus on the cross. The explanation was that the Jews did not have the right to use the death penalty, but we know that did not stop them when they wanted to execute someone. It may have been illegal but they did it anyway.

But the cross? They wanted Jesus to be executed on the cross. The cross was necessary to make an example of Jesus.

Do you think that the spectacle of the cross had a role to play in the "fullness of time"?

Somehow stoning or beheading or being shot with arrows or being stabbed or being strangled or drowned or any other way that man has devised to administer capital punishment simply does not carry the impact of the cross.

The symbolism is not there. "If I be lifted up…" lifted up for all the world to see. Of all the ways man has devised to execute those who do not fit the norm, the cross had and still has the unique ability to be a symbol.

I suppose we could put swords on the front of our churches.

The Moslem world uses a scimitar on many flags.

We could wear a small bunch of arrows on a chain around our necks.

We could have a pile of rocks at the front of the church and use them as an altar.

Joshua set up twelve stones at Gilgal as a memorial to the crossing of the Jordan river. Samuel set up a stone and named it Ebenezar and said "Thus far the Lord has helped us."

(I wonder how many people sing the second verse of "Come, Thou Fount of Every Blessing" and have no idea what the words, "Here I raise mine Ebenezar," means?)

Perhaps in modern times we could use a noose or an electric chair or a gas cylinder or a syringe or even a rifle. A guillotine would make a nice symbol. It was designed as an instrument of mercy you know. It was sure, fast and efficient.

But no method of execution has the emotional impact of the cross.

It took time to die on a cross. There was time to be seen. Time to think. Time to wonder. Time to make arrangements for the care of family. Time to ask questions.

"My God, my God, why hast thou forsaken me?"

Dying on the cross was a public event. It was a shameful spectacle. The criminal was naked. The loin cloth that we see on the crucifixes in gothic churches is an accommodation to the morals of a later time.

It was the custom to ridicule the dying man. They said:

> *"He saved others; he cannot save himself. Let the Messiah, the King of the Jews come down from the cross now, so that we may see and believe."*

Mark 15:31-32

The pain from crucifixion was extreme. Not only the pain of having nails driven through his feet and hands but he was beaten and abused. Death came slow. Sometimes criminals would live two or three days before they finally died.

So I wonder if the "Lifted up" aspect of the cross; the "up for the world to see" fact of the cross; the public spectacle of the cross was what made it "In the fullness of time."

I don't know. But I do know that even now, almost 2000 years later the cross is the symbol for the love of God.

> *"This is my commandment that you love one another as I have loved you. No one has greater love than this, to lay down one's life for one's friends."*

John 15:12-13

His Wounds

"Then the same day at evening, being the first day of the week, when the doors were shut where the disciples were assembled for fear of the Jews, came Jesus and stood in the midst, and saith unto them, Peace be with you. And when he had so said, he showed them his hands and his side."

John 20:19 and 20

The disciples were afraid.
Who wouldn't be afraid?
Who could be trusted?

What if they did believe Mary?
What if he was alive?
What then?

They could deal with death.
But resurrection?
How could they deal with resurrection?

He came to them and said,
"Peace be with you!"
And he showed them his wounds.

A week later they were still afraid.
They were still confused.
They were in the same room with the doors locked.

They did not feel peace.
They did not know what to do with peace.
They were afraid.

And he came again and said,
"Peace be with you!"
And he showed them his wounds.

He had a resurrected body
But he kept the wounds.
Why did he keep the wounds?

> Dietrich Bonheoffer said, "Only the suffering
> God can help us."

There was no salvation without the suffering.
There was no resurrection without the wounds.

Jesus did not hide his wounds.
Jesus did not hide his pain.
Jesus did not hide his suffering.

Jesus brought peace through his death.

The love of God is shown to the world by the wounds of Jesus.

Feed My Sheep

"Lovest thou me? Feed my sheep."

John 21:17

When the whole world had stopped looking for Jesus, Jesus came looking for those he loved.

To Mary he said, "Why weepest thou?"
> Are we, like Mary, so concerned with our problems,
> That we can not see him when we see him?

To the ten in a closed room he said, "Peace to you".
> Are we like the ten, so afraid that we are paralyzed,
> And do not consider looking for him?

To Thomas he said, "be not faithless.."
> Are we like Thomas, so full of doubt,
> That we can not believe the good news?

To the men on the Emmaus road, he said, "Why are ye troubled?'
> Are we like the men on the road, so absorbed
> by today's events,
> That we are not able to feel the divine presence
> among us?

To those who went fishing, he said, "Come and dine."
> Are we like the fishermen, so busy in our tasks,
> That we are hesitant to join the Lord at the
> table?

To Peter he said, "Do you love me? Feed my sheep."
> Are we like Peter, so filled with guilt and regret,
> That we are hesitant to follow him wherever
> he leads?

Lord give us the strength we need to trust you and follow you,
No matter where you lead, no matter what you call us to do.

Imperfection

Imperfection is all around us!
Everywhere!

We must not allow ourselves to be dominated by the imperfect.
Remember that our hope for the perfect is the very means
by which we recognize the imperfect.

If we did not know what is best,
Or if we did not care what is best,
We would not be in such a desperate struggle.

Faith in,
And hope for improvement
Is the essence of what traditional Christians call salvation.

The Good News is that we do not have to remain as we are!
      Racked by guilt,
      Paralyzed by fear.

We can improve,
And it is love that provides the courage to challenge the
imperfect

And live with it.

The imperfect in many cases can be dealt with,
And in any case it can be lived with,
But we must not fool ourselves,
It will never go away.

To be human means that imperfection is a part of life,
But to be loved means that imperfection can be faced with
courage.

The fact that God loves us and understands our imperfection
is what theologians call Justification!

The goal of love is,
        To redeem,
        To improve,
        To make right,
        To embrace,
        To cherish,
        To celebrate joy

And all of this takes hard work
And massive risks!

This is what we have been taught by scripture.
God in Christ brought love to mankind,
And it took
        Hard work,
        Massive risks,
        And total sacrifice,

And that is what history calls the Cross!

It is not what we have been,
Or what we are,
But what we can be that makes the difference.

What we can be;
Changed by the love of God;
Sanctified by His love flowing through us.

We are becoming,
We will always be becoming,
Which means that we haven't made it yet,

We will never be perfect,
We will always have to deal with the imperfect.
We will never stop loving.

H ope

The Christian message is hope!

We hope for the future.
Therefore, we prepare
By living today
In the confidence
Of what we believe
And in the expectation
That tomorrow
Will bring
A closer relationship
To those we love
To those who love us
To God.

We are what we have been becoming!

Help

What do I do, Lord
When I have done my very best
And it is not good enough?

Is it the demands of others
That set the standards
That I am incapable of meeting?

Or do I set the standards
That are impossible to meet
And thus set myself up for the fall?

Where is that famous bootstrap
By which I am supposed
To pull myself up?

Why is it that when
I am down here on the floor of the elevator
I can never find the up button?

Why is it that when it is one of my friends
Who is caught in the whirlpool
I can always see an easy rescue?

Or does the rescue look easy
Because I do not know the power
Of the force that is pulling them down?

Where are you Lord
When the magnitude of my despair
Short circuits all avenues of escape?

Where are you Lord?
I am waiting because that is all I can do.
I am trusting you Lord because only you can save me.

Thank you Lord for all you have done in the past.
Thank you Lord for the patience you are giving me now.
Thank you Lord for what you are going to do!

One Small Candle

"...Our salvation is neared than when we believed. The night is far spent, the day is at hand: let us therefore cast off the works of darkness, and let us put on the amour of light, Let us walk honestly, as in the day;"

Romans 13:11-13

The scripture we read at this time of the year looks forward to a better life. Let us look forward in hope!

Yogi Berra was quoted, when late in his carrier he was moved to play in the outfield,

"It gets late early out here".

Sometimes it seems like it is late, it looks like hope is fading away.

We live in a city where even before the end of the year we have recorded over 200 homicides.

Chemotherapy, Alzheimer's, pain, stress and death makes it seem like the dark night is still with us.

But, Paul reminds us that even though the night is not over the day is coming when the light will prevail.

Isaiah declares that the day of the Lord will come.
Isaiah dares us to hope.

> *"Come let us walk in the day of the Lord."*

> *Isaiah 2:5*

Let us walk in whatever light we have –
even if it is one small candle.

Let us use it to guide our footsteps.
Let us use it to light the way for others.

It may be just one small candle
but it is the light we have been given.

Let us use it to the glory of the Lord.

Horror Of Horrors

*"But when they believed Phillip, they were baptized,
both men and women."*

Acts 8:12

"Phillip was causing trouble in the church! He
was out of bounds!"

Stephen Cook

Phillip was not only preaching to the Samaritans, they accepted
the Gospel and "Horror of Horrors" Phillip baptized them!

Regardless of what the Christians in Jerusalem thought, God
had no respect for the wall they had built – no matter how high
and how secure they thought it was.

They sent Peter and John to straighten things out. But "Horror
of Horrors" when they laid hands on the Samaritans the Spirit
came upon them.

The good news is that the Spirit of God has descended upon us - no matter how formal and ritualistic we might be.

God has work for us to do and the Spirit will empower us to do it.

Let the Spirit move.
Be open to new power.
Get ready for the Spirit.

The Spirit of God wants to live in you and empower you to do a new and wonderful ministry in the Kingdom of God.

Are you open?
Are you willing?
Are you ready?

There is no limit to the power of the Holy Spirit.

"Horror of Horrors", your life might be radically changed!

Using Little Faith

"If ye had the faith as a grain of mustard seed, ye might say to this sycamore tree, Be thou plucked up by the root and be thou planted in the sea; and it should obey you."

Luke 17: 5-6

O ye of little faith!

What difference does it make that you possess a "Little Faith"?

Remember "Horton and the Who".

"A person's a person, no matter how small."
"There's a tiny person on that speck that needs my help!"

Even if your faith is as small as a mustard seed it is a significant amount of faith.

All things are relevant and faith as small as a mustard seed is an enormous mount of faith compared to the person has no faith.

Remember, little things can make a great difference in the Kingdom of God.

A mazing Grace

...."A man went out early in the morning to hire laborers... for a penny a day. And he went out about the third hour. And said go ye also into the vineyard. And he went out in the sixth hour and the ninth hour and about the eleventh hour. They every man received a penny.

So the first shall be last and the last first:"

Matthew 20:1-16

This is the most offensive parable Jesus told.
It is just not fair!

But:

Do not underestimate the Grace of God.
God's grace is complete, absolute.
He will give it to anyone he chooses,
And he chooses to give it to everyone,
Regardless!

That is Amazing Grace!

God is rumbling through the "Hood" looking for workers in the Kingdom.

It can be the "Upper Class Hood".
It can be the "Middle Class Hood".
It can be the "Poverty Class Hood."

In any case he is looking for workers in the Kingdom.

We are all loved by the same God.
We all receive the same grace.

God is not fair.
(Fair means that you get what you deserve.)
God gives his grace to all.
Regardless of circumstances.

God's grace is amazing.
Too amazing for our narrow and hardened hearts to understand.

Regardless of when God comes through your "Hood".
Looking for workers in his kingdom,
GET ON THE BUS!

Get ready to work.
Get ready to serve.
Get ready to love.

When I was about 14 year old we lived in a suburb of Chattanooga, Tennessee. In the early summer a farmer, in his old stake bed truck, would rumble through the neighborhood blowing his horn. We would run out to the

road and climb on. We rode the truck to the strawberry fields just north of the city. We picked strawberries (I think they paid us 5 cents a quart.) and made a little pocket change. Enough for a RC cola and a moon pie. We were glad to get a little paying work and the farmer got some cheap labor.

Andrew

Taking Sides

"Let love be without dissimulation. Be kindly affectioned one to another with brotherly love."

Romans 12: 9 and 10

Paul never discounted reality.
He was well aware of disharmony within the church.
He had every reason to be sarcastic and disappointed.

The question was then
And the question now,
Is not, "Is God on our side?"
The question is are we on God's side?

And which side is God's side?
It is the side of compassion.
It is the side of sacrifice.
It is the side of love.

God is on the side of those,
Who are suffering,
Who are in pain,
Who have been abused.

The wisdom of the world is to win at all costs.
The wisdom of God is to love regardless.

What is the challenge to Christians?
Are we up to the challenge?
Can we love regardless?

A Speechless God

"Unto thee, O Lord, do I lift up my soul. Oh my God, I trust in thee: let me not be ashamed, let not mine enemies triumph over me."

Psalms 25:1-2

It is only three days after five police officers were assassinated in Dallas, Texas.

Twenty-eight days after forty-nine people were killed in a nightclub in Orlando, Florida.

There is evil in this world.
There has always been evil in this world.

How do we pray?
What can we do?

Right before the Apostle Paul assures us of the love of God in Romans 8:35:

"Who shall separate us from the love of Christ? Shall tribulation, or distress, or persecution, or famine, or nakedness, or peril, or sword?"

He confesses that we do not know how to pray.

"for we know not what we should pray for as we ought."

But he goes on to say:

"But the Spirit itself maketh intercession for us with groanings which cannot be uttered."

Romans 8:26

Sometimes there are no words:
A groan,
A cry,
A scream?

A caring God!
A speechless God!
Even God is speechless in the depth of his caring for us!

We know we are your children,
But, we have limits.

How do we live in responsible love with all people?
How do we learn to live within our limits,
And let God be God?

We confess our vulnerability,
And trust that somehow you will bring order out of chaos.

The Strategic Table

"But when thou makest a feast, call the poor, the maimed, the lame. the blind: And thou shalt be blessed."

Luke 14:13

We have all known the zealous hostess who went to great lengths to be sure the seating arrangement at the banquet was correct. A great amount of energy and contemplation went into who sat by whom.

The world is very concerned about who is in and who is out. Who is in front and who is behind.

Jesus said that no one is out – everyone is in!
We are all invited to the table of God.

There is never a second class seat at God's table.
There is no "head" table.

God has a "Non- Ranking" table.
God is equally at all places at the table.
God is seated beside every person.

No one is left out.
No one is uninvited.
No one is graded down.

Every one of the children of God is one for whom Jesus died.

Where is our respect for others?
Where is the culture of love?

Jesus Math

"Neither pray I for thee alone but for them also which shall believe in me through the word. That they all may be one, as thou father art in me and I in thee, that they also may be one."

John 17:20-21

Jesus does not use the same math as the rest of us.

One + One + One + Others (Us?) = One!

Jesus was praying for not only for his disciples but for all future disciples.

The question is:
Who is praying for you?
Who are you praying for?

It is vitally important that prayers go with us when we go out into the world to serve the Master.

It is vitally important that our prayers go with our friends as they go out into the world to serve the master.

> This is children's day and the front of the church is full of beautiful, intelligent, precocious children. Remember – we are training some other church's ministers and teachers and servants. Very few of these children will remain in this church. Jobs and spouses and other demands will move them out to other churches.
>
> Stephen Cook

When they go –
Be sure they go with our love.
Be sure they go with our prayers.

Say Something Tell Somebody

> *"he hath chosen us in him before the foundation of the world, that we should be holy and without blame before him in love."*
>
> *Ephesians 1:4*

God chose to love us with an undiminishing love long before we ever existed.

It has nothing to do with what we do or what we do not do. God loves us regardless.

It was for us that Jesus Christ came into the world.
It was for us that Jesus Christ died on the cross.
It was for us that Jesus Christ was raised from the dead.
It is for us that Jesus Christ will come again.

That is the Gospel!
That is what we need to tell the world.

There is a current saying in this fractured time we live in:

If you see something, say something.

Perhaps we should sanctify the saying:

If you know something,
    (If you know the love of God)
Tell somebody!

The church needs to speak up.

We need to speak up.

Markers

"Show us thy mercy, O Lord, and grant us thy salvation."

Psalms 85:7

Psalms 85 is a perpetually appropriate prayer.

Stephen Cook

What you pray for and what you dream about and what you get are never exactly the same.

Life's adventures may take you many places and when (or if) you get back home it will not be the same.

Things change.

There are times that put markers on our lives and everything else is remembered as before or after our markers.

Marriage
School
Jobs

Children
Sickness
Diverse
Death

When life takes an unexpected turn we are prone to pray for a way back to the way it was.

But:

Life must go forward.

"Grace hath bro't me safe thus far, and grace will lead me home".

John Newton

It is not "Back Home" it is "To Home".

Pause long enough to hear what God has to say. Remember that his

Steadfast love
Faithfulness
Righteousness
and Peace

Are guaranteed.

Then, move on to whatever the future might be.

Go with God!

The Difficult Task

"Don't worry about anything; instead pray about everything. Tell God what you need and thank him for all he has done. Then you will experience God's peace."

Philippians 4:9 NLT

Do not worry?
What is Paul talking about?

If you are human at all you worry.
If you care at all you worry.

That does not mean that you do not ask questions.
That does not mean that you do not struggle with imperfection.

But in everything keep doing the work of the church.

That was true in Philippi and that is true in Memphis.

The work of the church in this little corner of God's Kingdom is important. We are better together, as a church, than we are as individuals.

Keep on doing the ministry of the gospel:

> *"Whatsoever things are true,*
> *Whatsoever things are honest,*
> *Whatsoever things are just,*
> *Whatsoever things are pure,*
> *Whatsoever things are lovely,*
> *Whatsoever things are of good report,*
> *Do these things and the God of peace will be with you."*
>
> *Philippians 4:8 and 9*

Let the ministry of the Gospel fill your life so that there is no place for worry.

Grief

"But I would not have you to be ignorant, brethren, concerning them that are asleep, that ye sorrow not, even as others that have no hope. For if we believe that Jesus died and rose again, even so them which sleep in Jesus will God bring with him.

I Thessalonians 4:13 and 14

We are all touched by grief. Death is the only common experience we all have except birth. We are not aware of our birth but all of us are aware of death.

Today is one week after 26 people were killed at the Sutherland Springs Baptist Church in Texas. In the span of two weeks we have had two of the deadliest mass shooting in the recent history of our nation.

There is no way we can feel the pain of the people of the Sutherland Springs Baptist Church but on the other hand the body count in our own city since January 1 is 3 ½ times the massacre in Texas.

Sometimes it feels like it is too much.

Paul does not say that we should not grieve.
And, Paul does not use any of the pathetic platitudes we so callously use.

"It was simply God's will."
"God needed another angel in his choir."
"Earth's loss but heaven's gain."

It is important that we grieve. We should grieve. We must grieve.
But, we should not grieve as those who have no hope.

We do have hope. Jesus died but he rose again.
We are not left to live alone in a vast world of loss and pain.

We are surrounded by the love of a God that embraces us and sustains us. And we are surrounded by fellow Christians who love us and care for us.

Grieve.
Grieve well.
Grieve completely.

Then get on with the ministry of the Gospel.

Nathanael In His Man Cave

"Jesus...findeth Phillip, and saith unto him, Follow me. Philip findeth Nathanael, and saith unto him, We have found him,...Jesus of Nazareth. And Nathanael said unto him, Can there any good thing come out of Nazareth?

Nathanael saith unto him, Whence knowest thou me? Jesus answered and said into him, Before that Phillip called thee, when thou wast under the fig tree, I saw thee."

John 1:43 – 48

Where?
From Nazareth?
No way! Not from Nazareth.

Everybody knows that nothing good can come out of Nazareth.
Nathanael was in the "Everybody" camp.
Phillip did not question. He simply believed.

Nathanael had preconceived beliefs.
Nathanael struggled.
He had questions.

He was convinced that he knew the truth.
He did not realize that all the truth he knew
Was not all the truth.

Jesus called Phillip who was anxious and eager to respond.
Jesus called Nathanael who was comfortable under his fig tree (Man Cave).
Jesus calls us regardless of whether we are eager to serve like Phillip,
Or whether we are comfortable under our fig tree (Man Cave or She Shed) like Nathanael.

Jesus calls us o'er the tumult of our life's wild, restless sea:
day by day His sweet voice soundeth saying, "Christian Follow Me."

Cecil Frances Alexander

Wait Upon The Lord

"But they that wait upon the Lord shall renew their strength: they shall mount up with wings as eagles; they shall run and not be weary; and they shall walk and not faint."

Isaiah 40; 31

Each year at the fund raising event for youth ministries the pastor auctions off a sermon. Whoever wins the bid gets to select a passage of scripture for the pastor to use in one of his sermons. Last year the winner chose Isaiah 40:31,

The pastor placed, on the top of the pulpit, a stack of 65 programs from funerals of members who have died since he became our pastor seven years ago.

There is a story about every person who died during that time. Many of the services included this passage from Isaiah 40.

Isaiah 40 is a turning point in the book of Isaiah. In Isaiah 40 we find a new beginning; a new hope. Isaiah begins to preach that Israel should not give up hope regardless of the circumstances.

Our God is:
> A God who is steadfast;
> A God who does not give up,
> A God who believes in his children.
> A God who is stronger than any enemy.

Listen to those who can remember.
Listen to those who have been through the battle of life.

Every person who is part of those 65 programs knows that,
> The storms of life will pass.
> The love of God endures.
> The power of God is sufficient.

God is not done yet.

Isaiah said, "Wait upon the Lord,
> Mount up with wings like eagles,
> Run and not be weary.
> Walk and not faint.

To paraphrase the man in the insurance commercial:

God knows a thing or two!

Awareness

When you feel that God is distant
And not involved in your life –
Rejoice!
Comfort is on its way.

The awareness of need
Is the first step to reconciliation.

God,
The hound of heaven,
Is constantly
Pursuing you,
Wooing you,
Calling you,
Into fellowship
And joy.

Praise the Lord.

Ego

God does not have the same ego problems we have.

God is not mocked.
God is not humiliated.
God does not lose face.
God is not embarrassed

Israel had to lose the ark before they could get over their superstitions about the ark.

God can always win when it is appropriate for him to win but he can also wait as long as necessary.

When Jesus died on the cross all was lost, or so it seemed, but in time, God's time, God's purpose was fulfilled.

God does not grieve over the loss of"things".

God grieves over the loss of love.
God grieves over the loss of loyalty.
God grieves over the loss of worship.

But he can
And he will wait for us.

Thank God.

The Velveteen Rabbit

"The most important things in life can not be defined by literalism.

It is:
   The roses,
   The love songs,
   The turkey dinner,
   The stained glass,
   The Christmas tree,
   The small gifts of tenderness.

That is what makes life real.

It is like the story of the Velveteen Rabbit.
The rabbit was real because the boy said so.
But not before all his hair had been loved off
And he had become lumpy and misshaped.

The thought about tenderness is from a sermon by Roger Lovette.

The thought about the Velveteen Rabbit is by Andrew.

Friends

"When Jesus saw their faith, he said to the sick of the palsy, Son, thy sins be forgiven thee."

"And immediately he arose, took up his bed, and went forth before them all:...."

Mark 2:5 and 2:11

His sins were forgiven because of their faith!

Their faith!

He was healed because of their faith!

Their faith!

Forgiveness came first.

Healing came later.

Healing without forgiveness in never enough.

Jesus was in the restoration business.

Jesus is still in the restoration business.

Restoration is always as much about forgiveness as it is about healing.

Sometimes restoration, forgiveness, healing comes with the help of your friends.

"When he saw their faith!

Their faith!

Never under estimate the power of your friends.

Never under estimate your power to help your friends.

E rasures

The erasures –
The crossed out words –
The X'd out paragraphs

They are so important,
They are the record of change,
They are the beginning of improvement.

> If there are no erasures
> there is no improvement.

The manuscript tells so much more than the finished page. The starts – the stops – the blind alleys – the deletions – the wrong turns – the turn arounds – the deliberate reversals of direction.

It is like the word picture from the Youraba language that Dr. Scott Patterson used to explain the concept of repentance.

> "A man who meets himself coming down the road."

Why do we hide the erasures?
Why do we leave out the blanked out words?
Why do we ignore the X'd out paragraphs?

They tell us so much.
They remind us that we have changed.
They encourage us to continue to make changes.

Erasures prepare us for growth in the Kingdom of God.

To Dwell In The Mystery

"To dwell in the mystery."
I used that phrase a long time ago in something I wrote.
To dwell in the mystery long enough to let the Holy Spirit do
his work.

Dwell, is almost as important a word as mystery.
Dwell, implies patience.
You can not dwell in a hurry.

Unhurried time,
Immersed in mystery,
Grounds you to the eternal.

Wait!
Who wants to wait?
Why not act?

Make a decision!
It is not as easy as it seems.
Waiting sometimes takes more strength than action.

Lord, give me patience.
Lord, give me wisdom.
Lord, let me dwell in your mystery.

About the Author

Andrew Smith, Architect by trade, consistent Christian by conviction has blended creativity and faith in this collection of his God encounters. His thoughts are linked like beads on a necklace: different shapes of poetry and prose all of which are grounded by reality and hope. Each arises from private experiences and from gathered congregations. Many are stirrings stimulated by messages delivered by his pastors.

A word of warning – some are sticky and may remain with the reader far beyond a single reading.

Andrew Smith graduated from high school in 1950 and joined the Navy. After the end of the Korean Conflict he began his study in architecture at Georgia Tech and received his BArch in 1961.

While he was in college he became the pastor of a small rural church just north of Atlanta called Dunwoody Baptist. He led the church to make several important and far reaching decisions.

Contrary to the expectations of the day, he did not feel a call to the professional ministry and began his career in architecture in 1961. His architectural practice has produced many types of buildings in over twenty states. He now serves as an associate principal with Self Tucker Architects in Memphis, Tennessee.

He married Mary Jo Mynatt in 1953. They have three children, three grandchildren and four great grand children.

They have been members of Second Baptist Church in Memphis since 1968.

Printed in the United States
By Bookmasters